Draw Stylish Dragon Tattoos For Girls And Boys

Drawing Dragon Tattoos Step-by-Step

Dragon Tattoos

By : Gala Publication

2

Published By :

Gala Publication
© Copyright 2015 – Gala Publication

ISBN-13: **978-1522707684**
ISBN-10: **1522707689**

Table of Contents

CHINESE DRAGON TATTOO

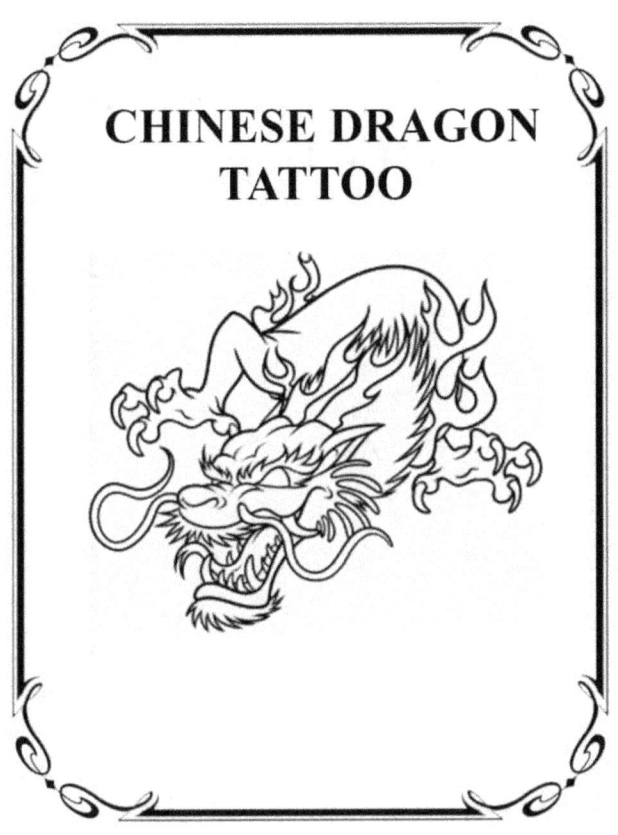

STEP 1

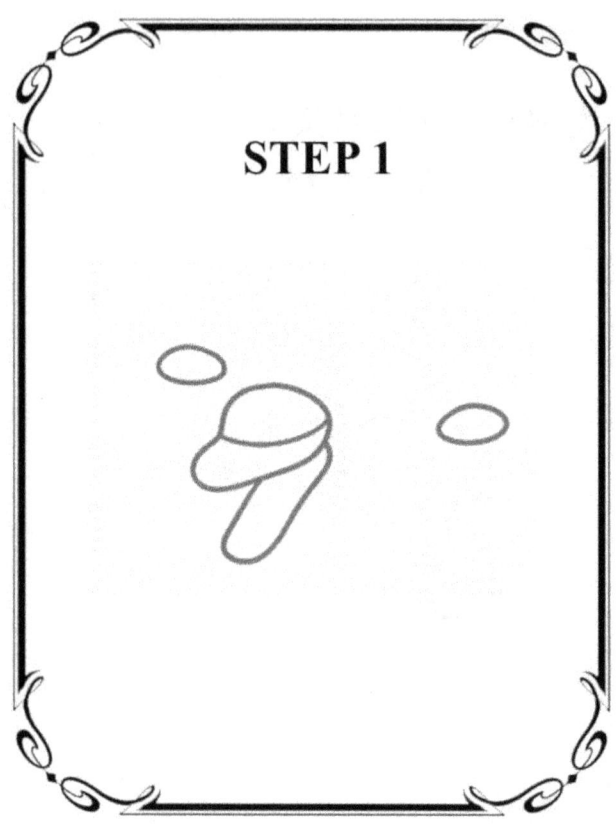

STEP 2

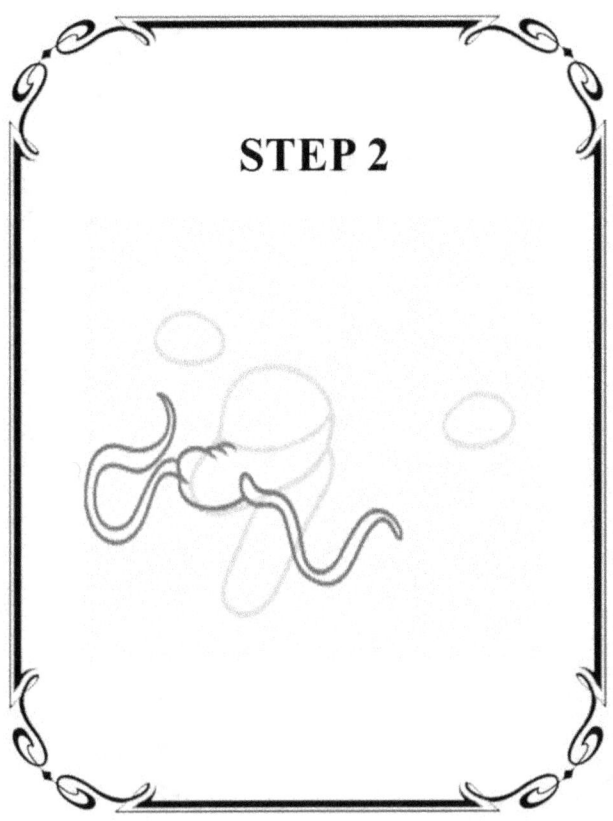

STEP 3

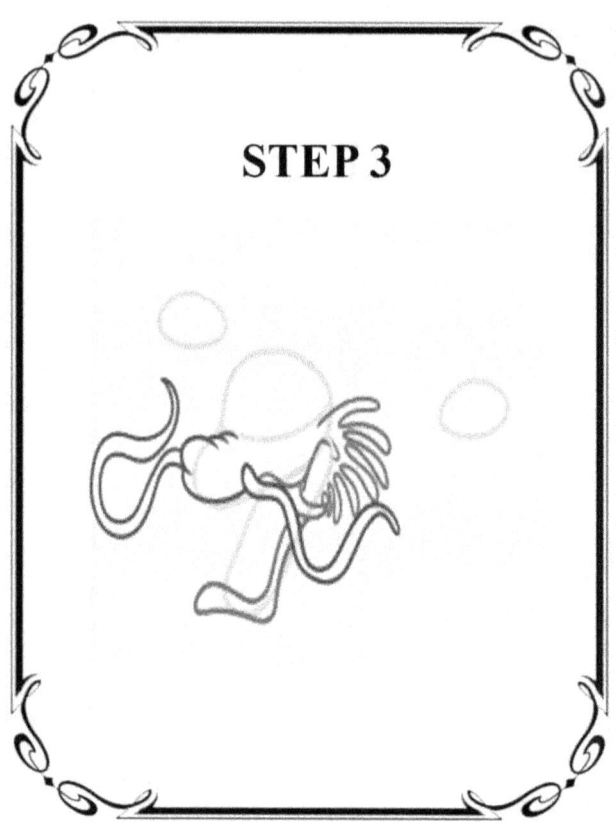

STEP 4

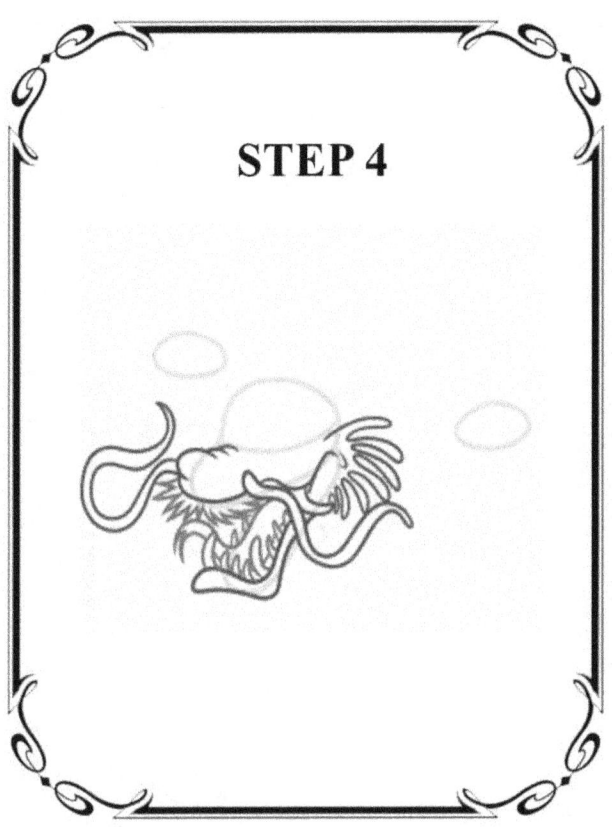

STEP 5

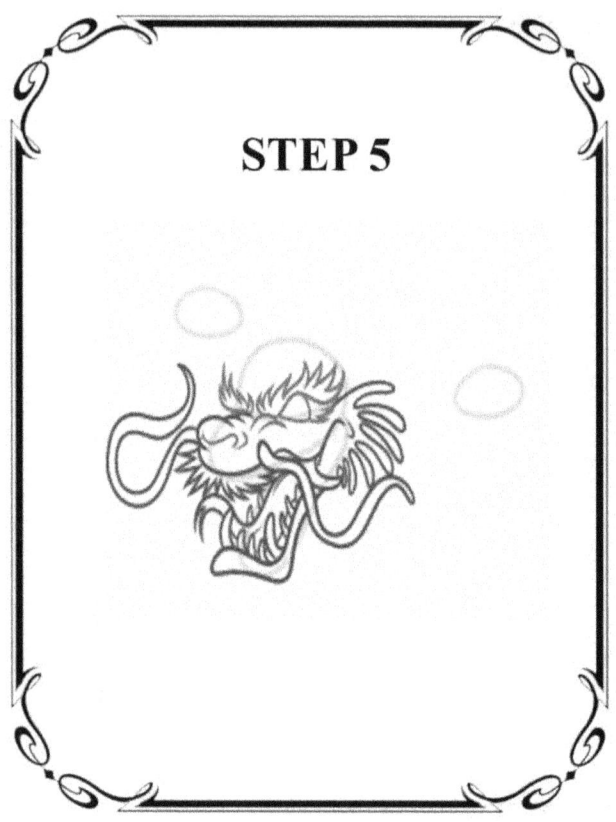

STEP 6

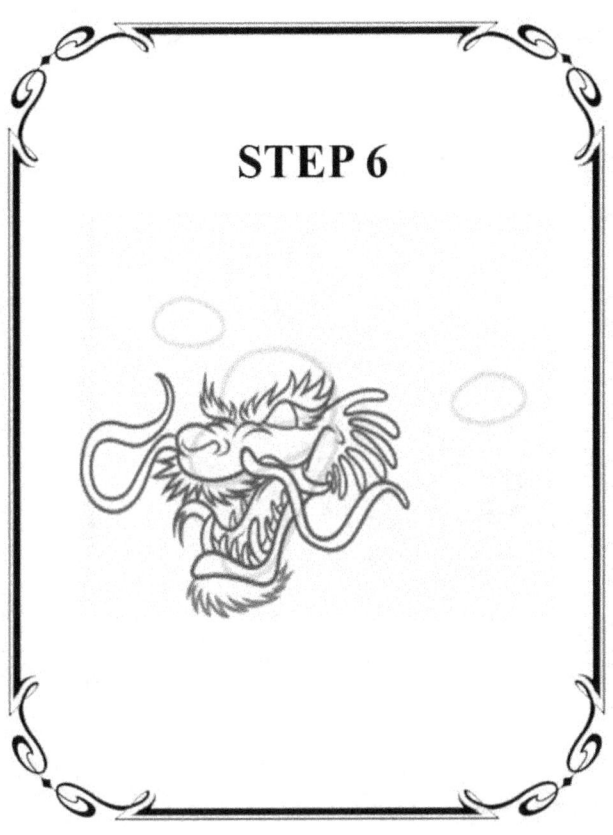

STEP 7

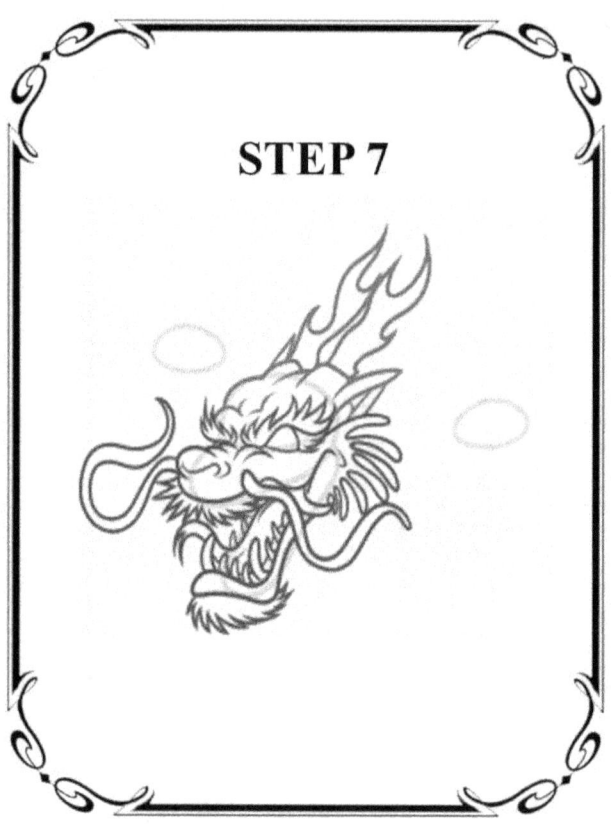

STEP 8

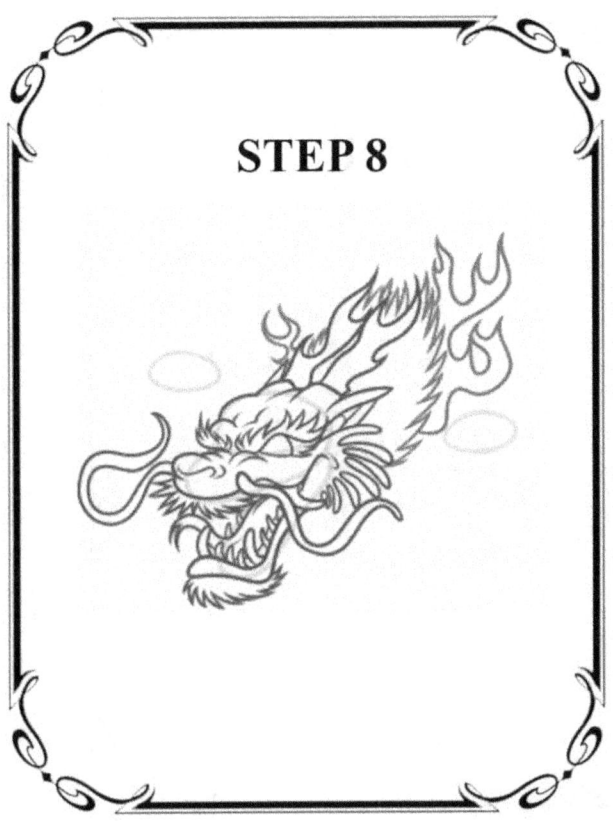

STEP 9

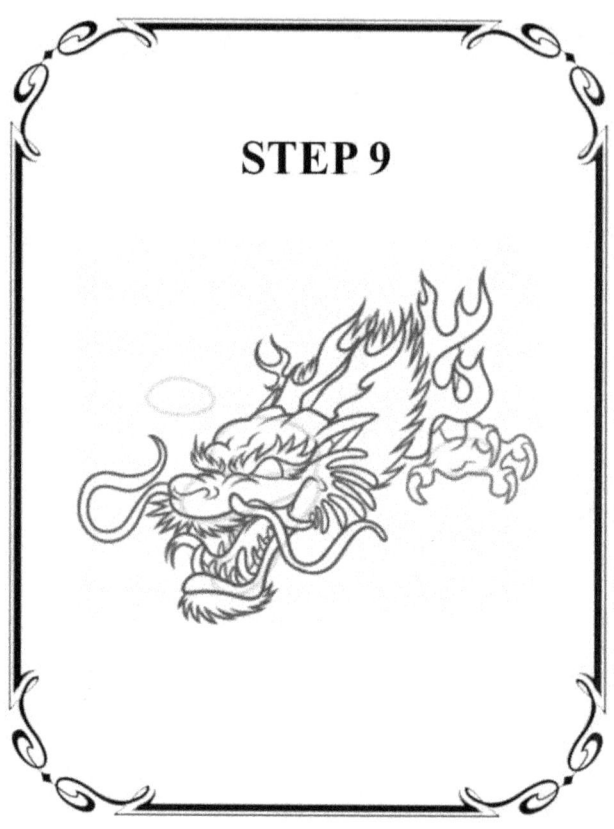

STEP 10

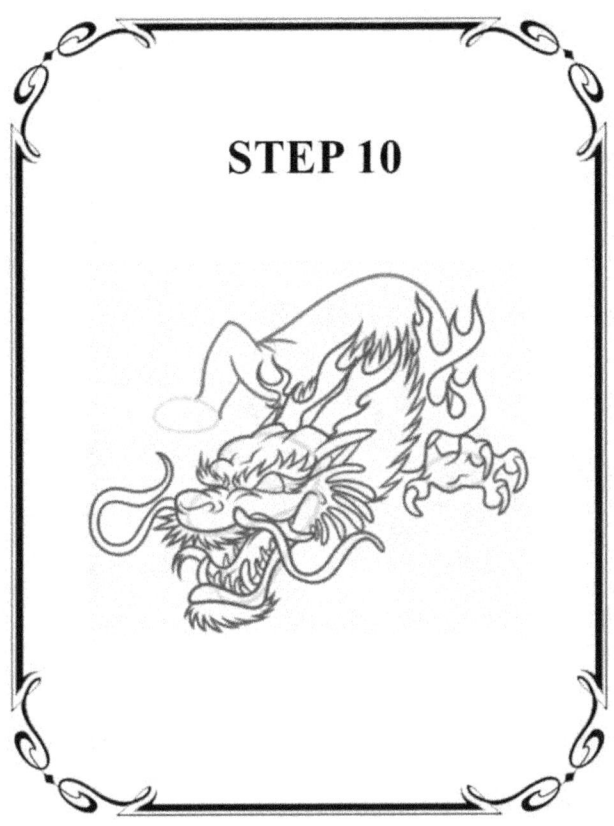

STEP 11

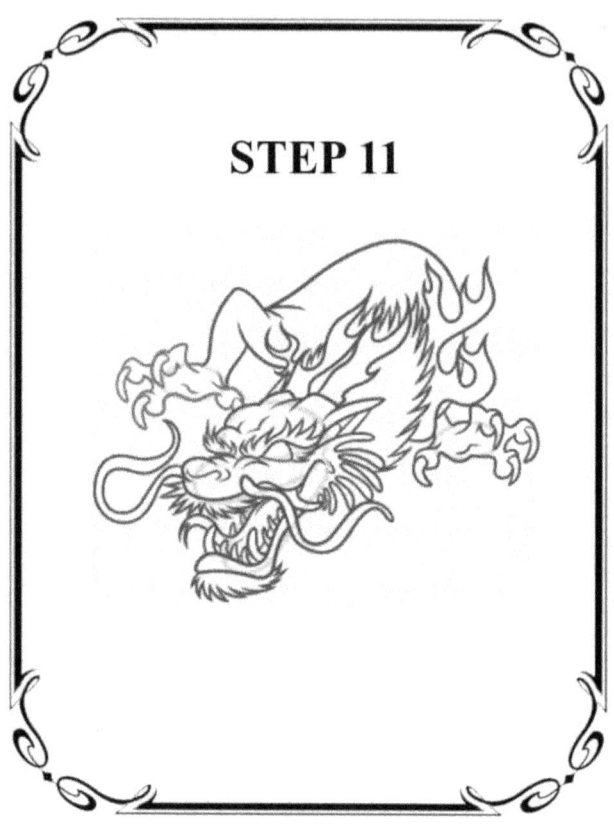

STEP 12

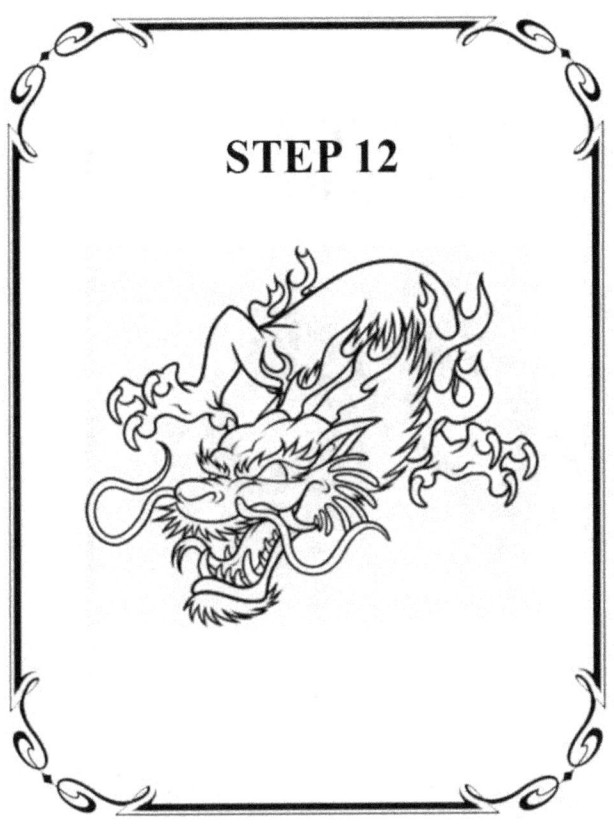

INFINITY DRAGON TATTOO

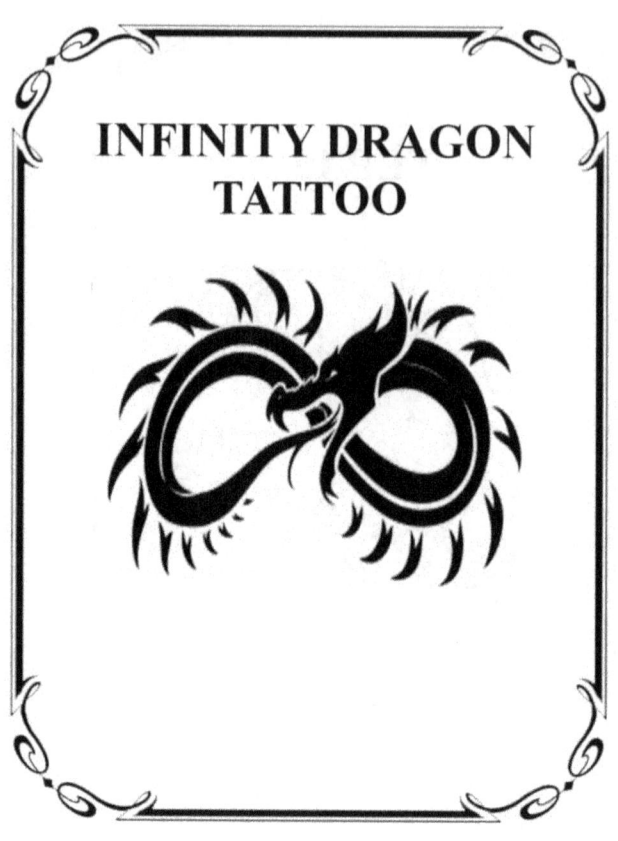

STEP 1

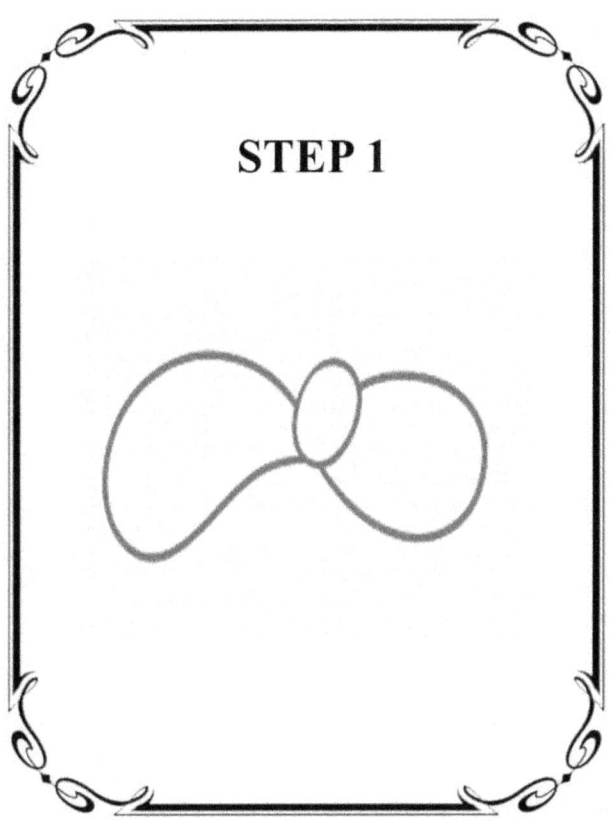

STEP 2

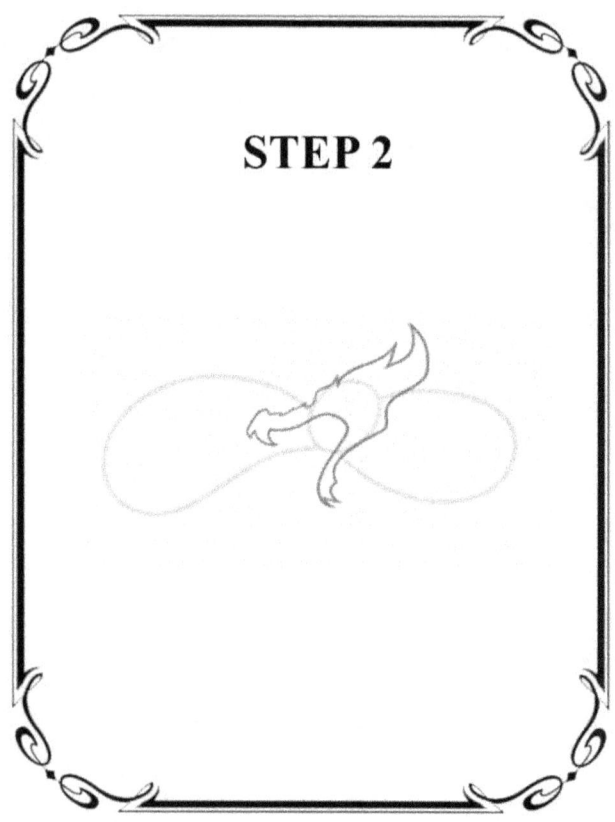

STEP 3

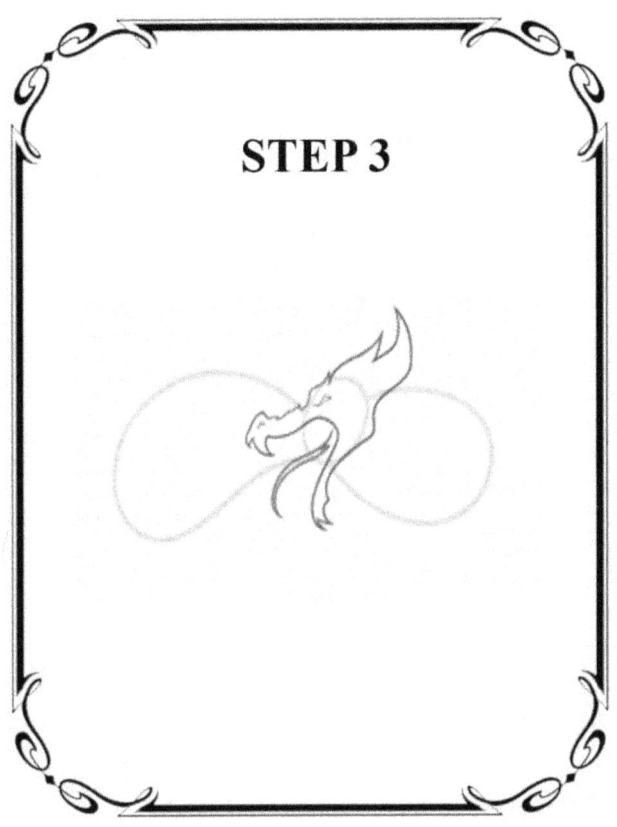

STEP 4

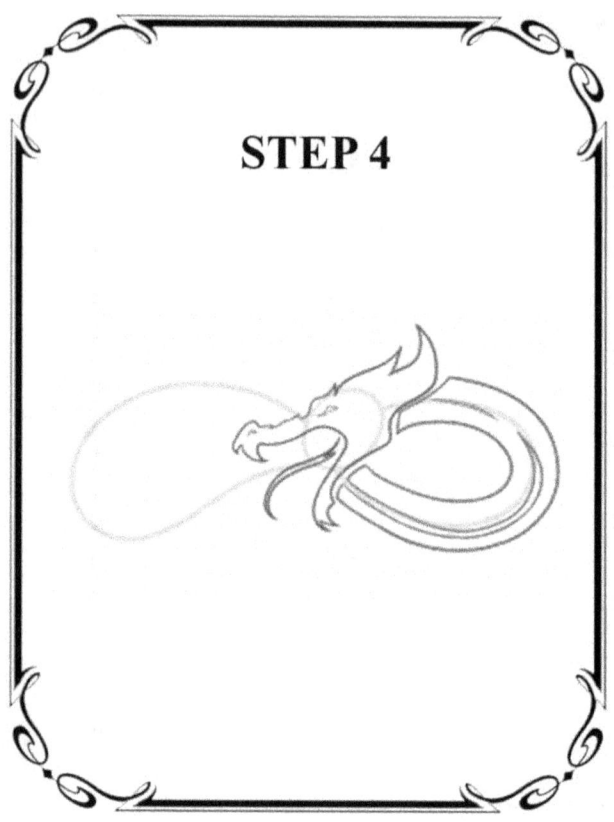

STEP 5

STEP 6

JAPANESE DRAGON TATTOO

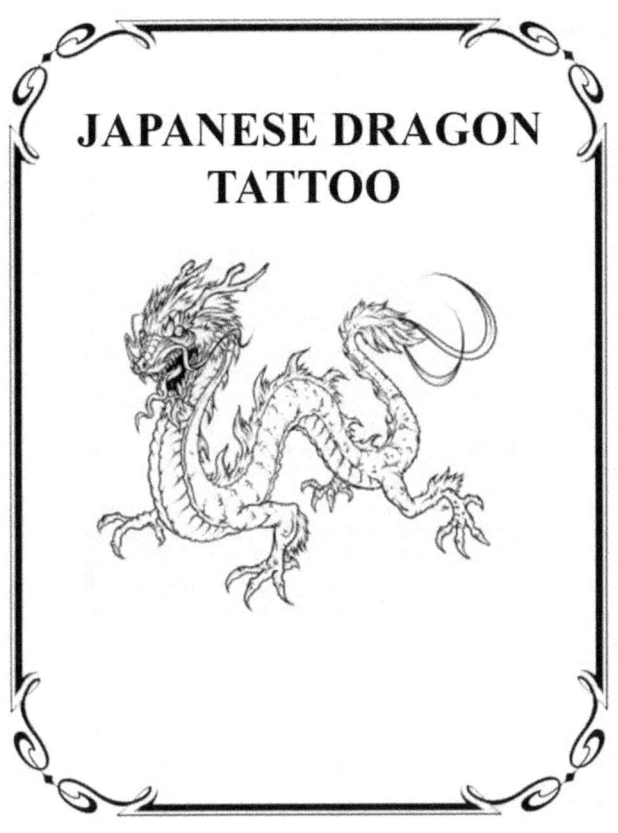

STEP 1

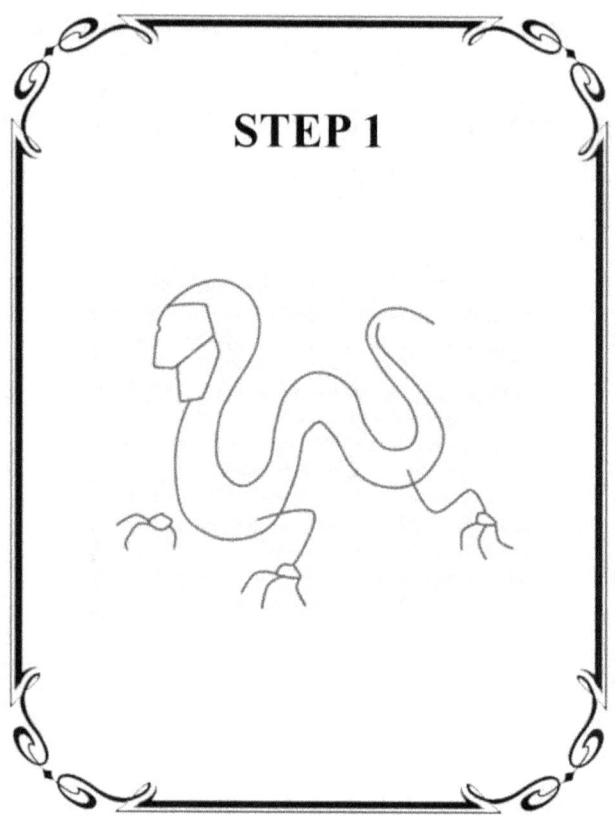

STEP 2

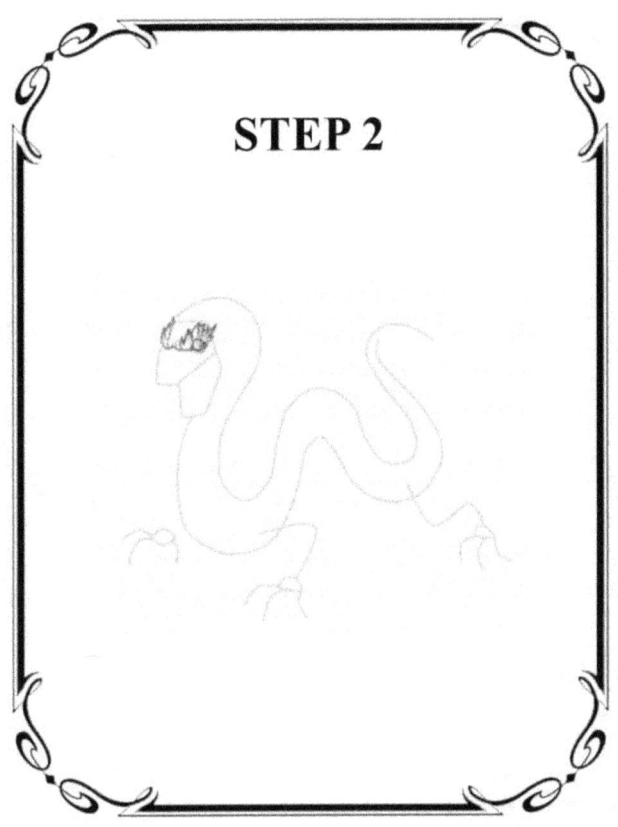

STEP 3

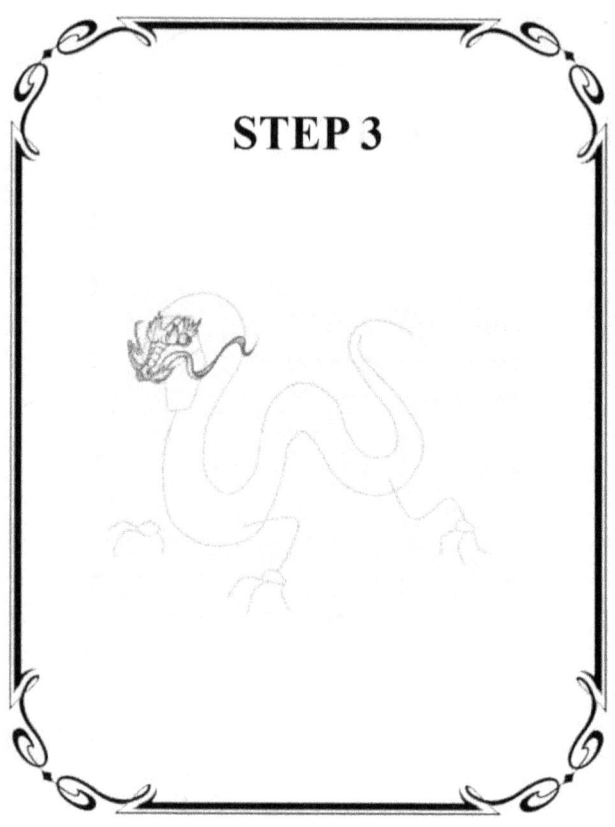

STEP 4

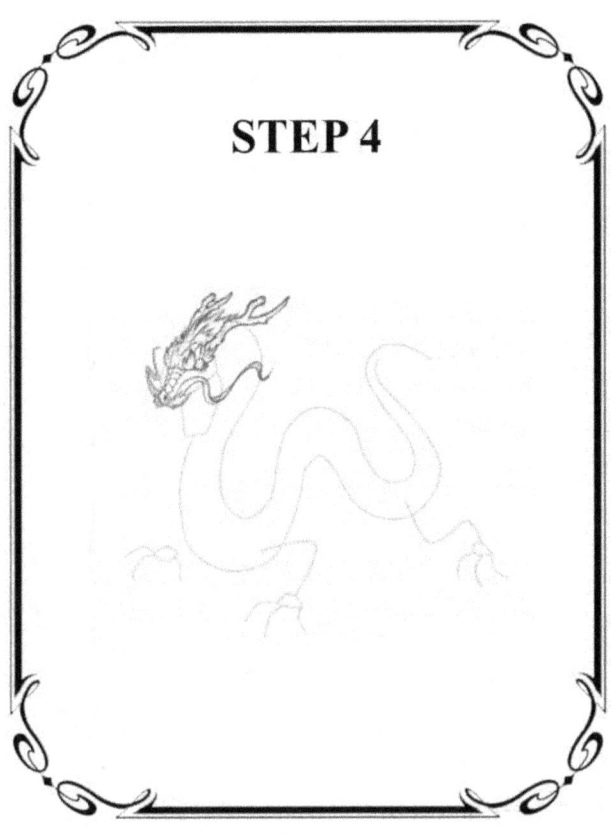

STEP 5

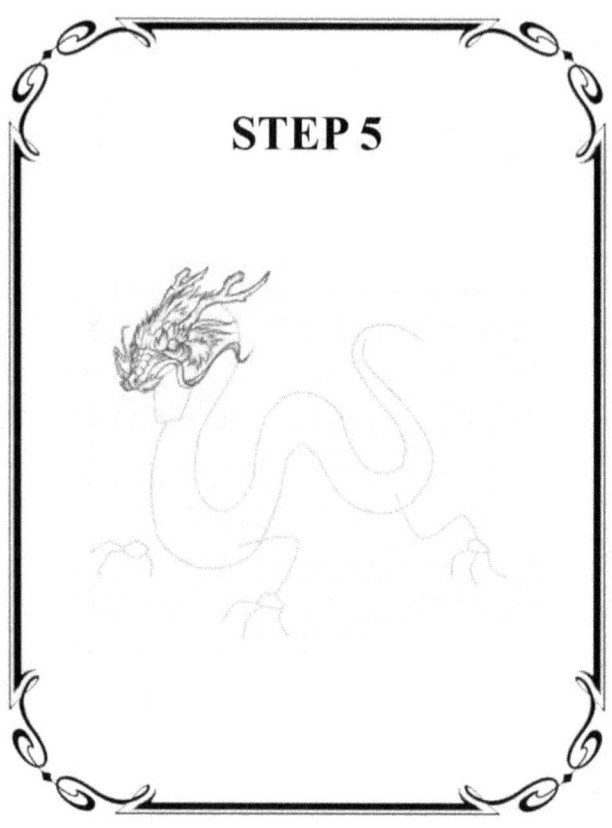

STEP 6

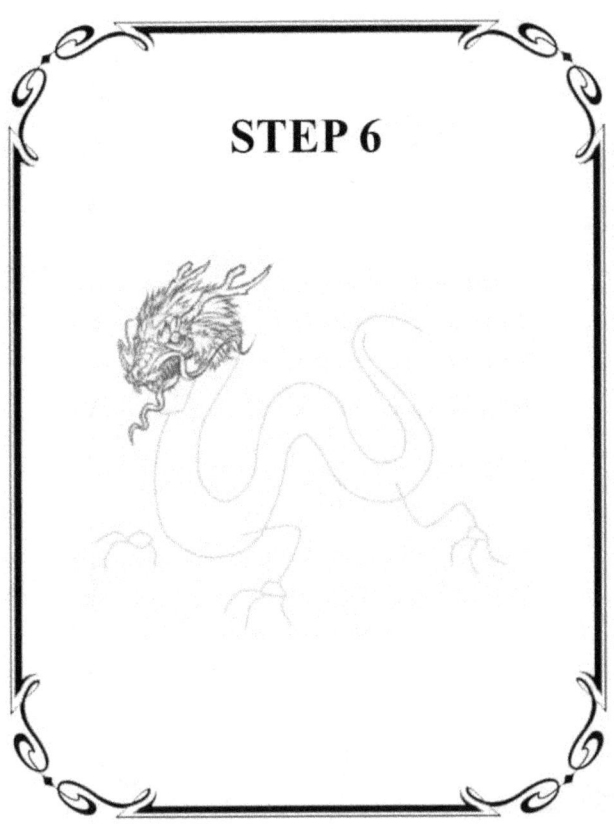

STEP 7

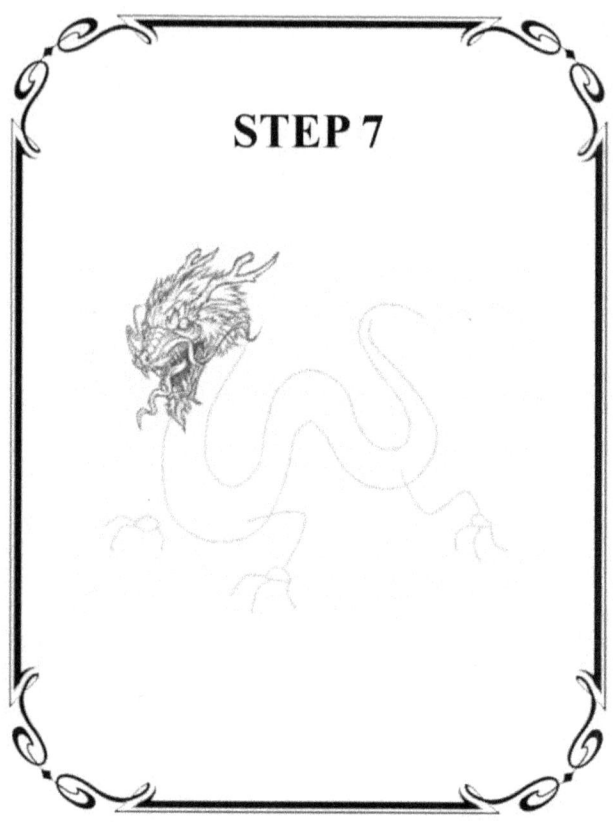

STEP 8

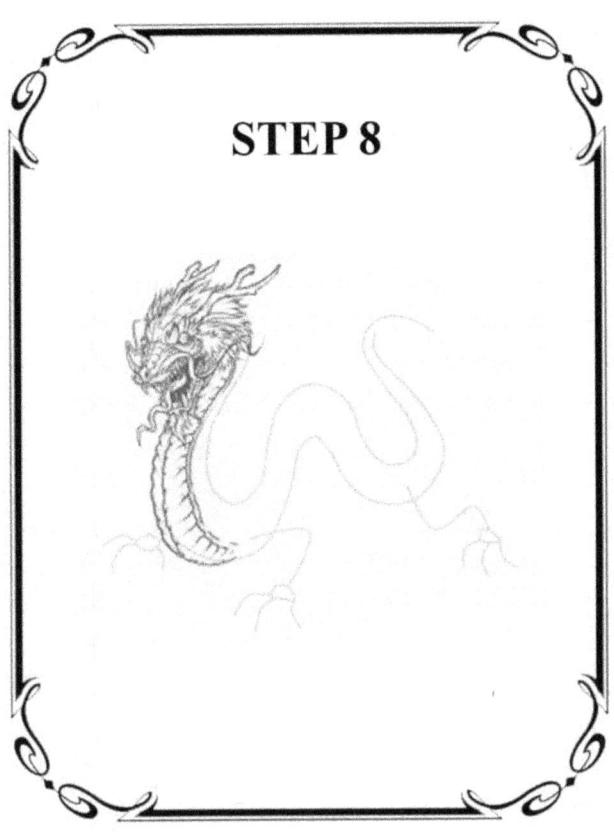

STEP 9

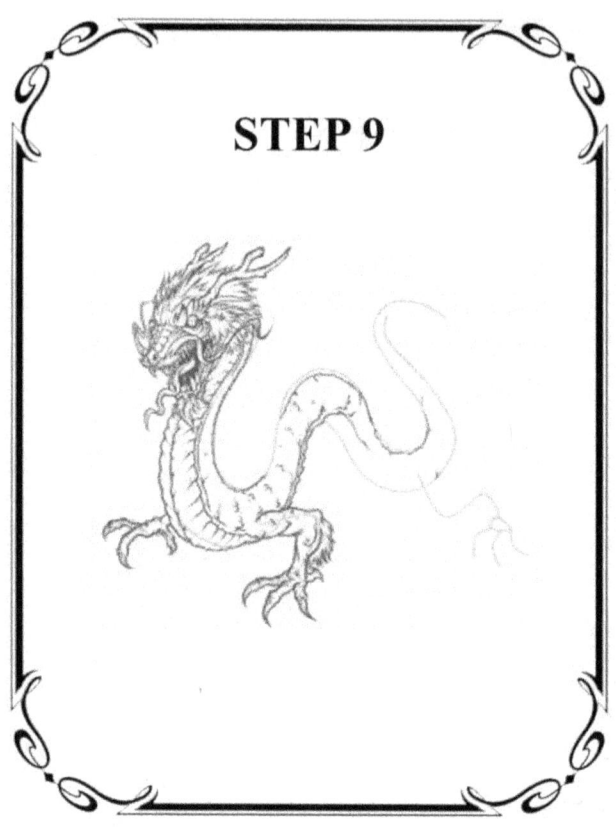

STEP 10

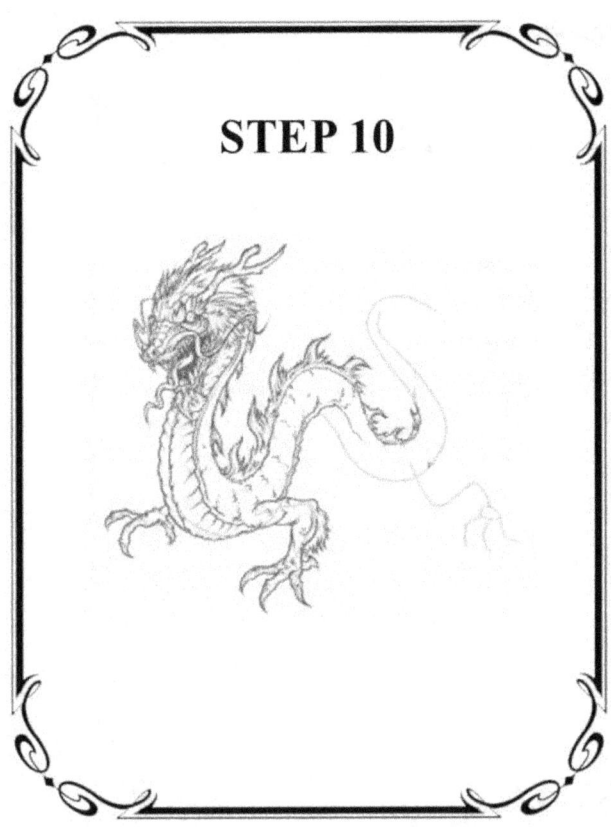

STEP 11

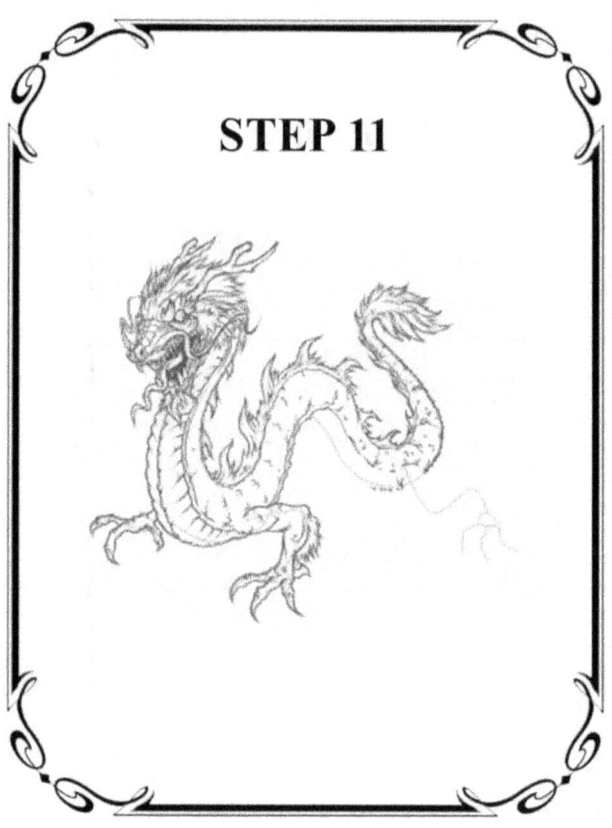

STEP 12

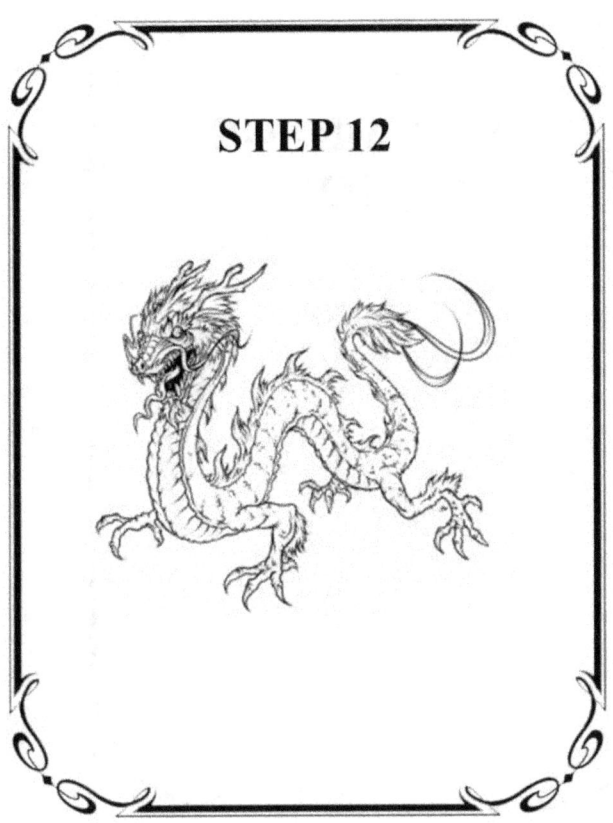

SIMPLE DRAGON TATTOO

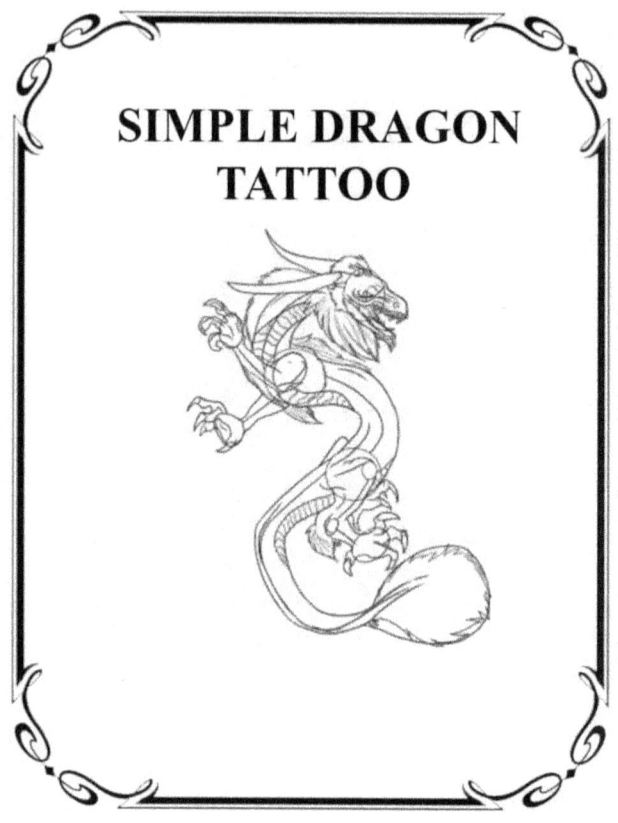

STEP 1

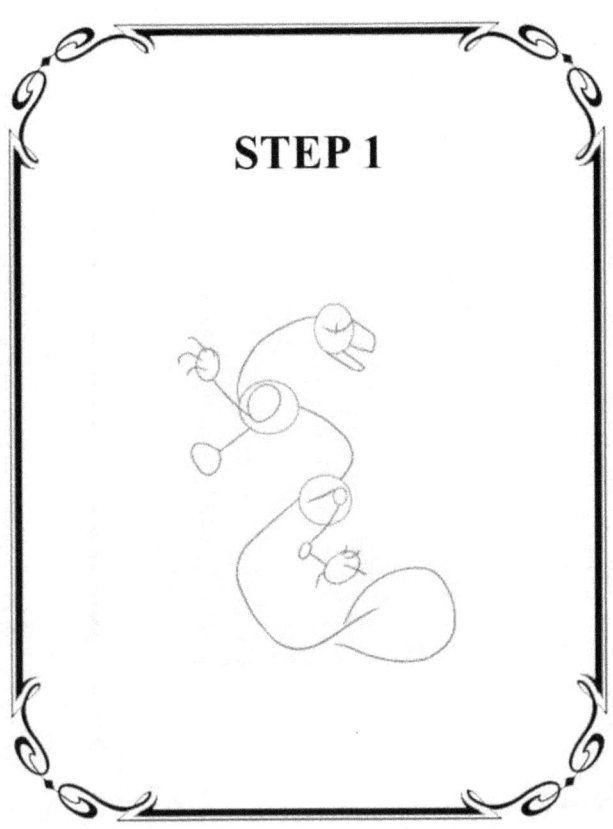

STEP 2

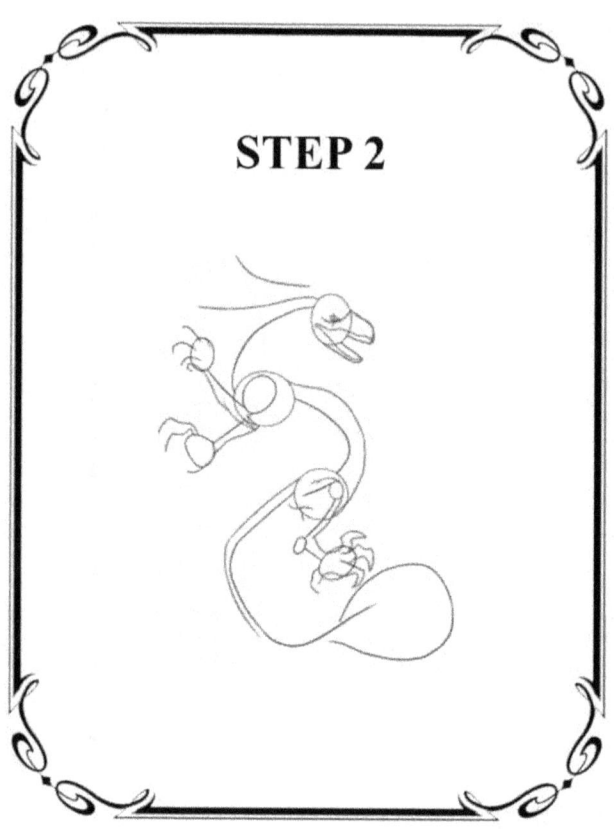

STEP 3

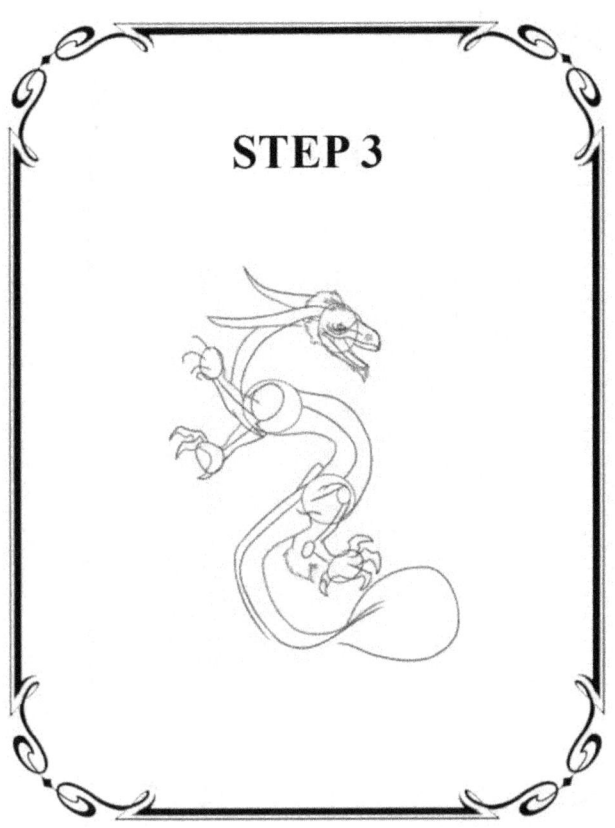

STEP 4

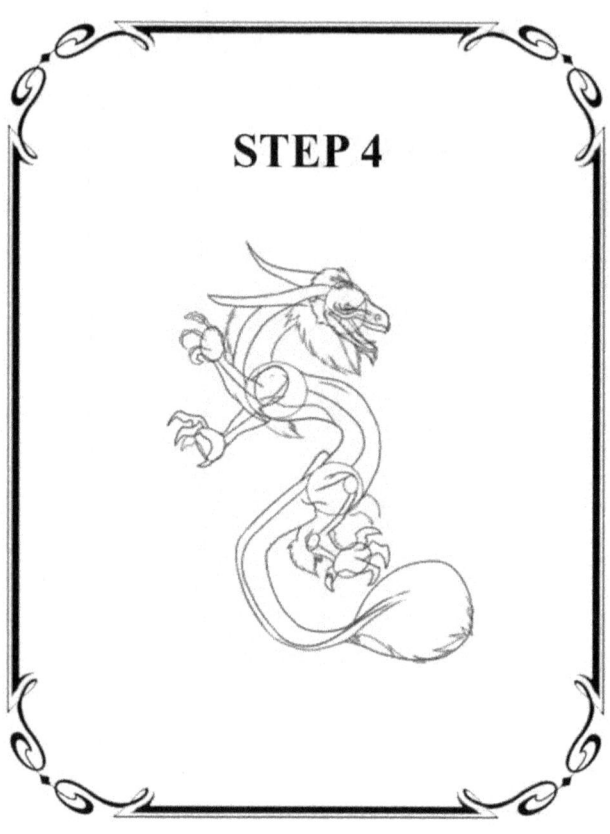

STEP 5

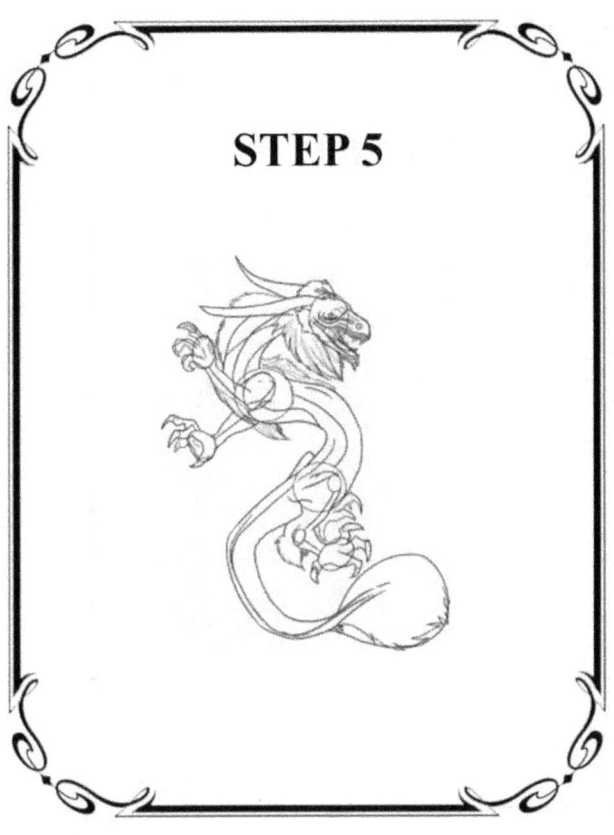

STEP 6

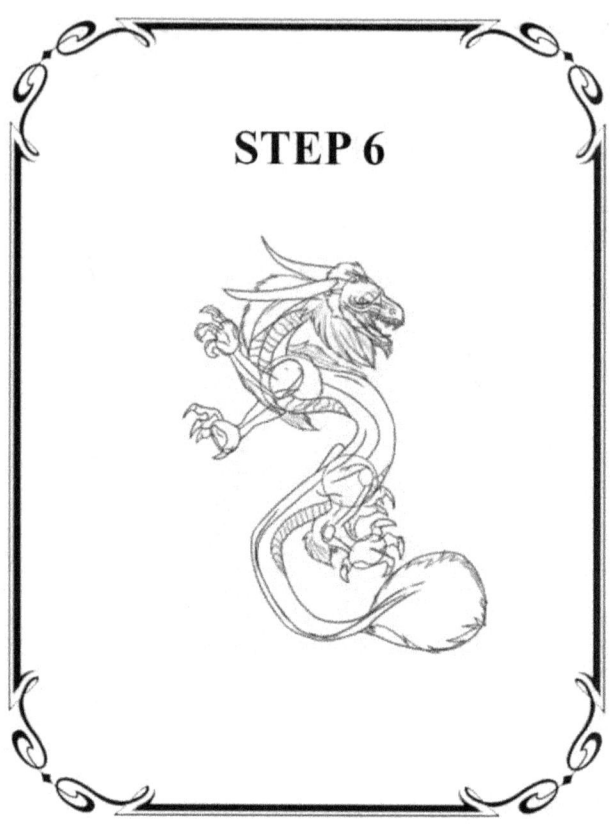

45

TRIBAL DRAGON TATTOO

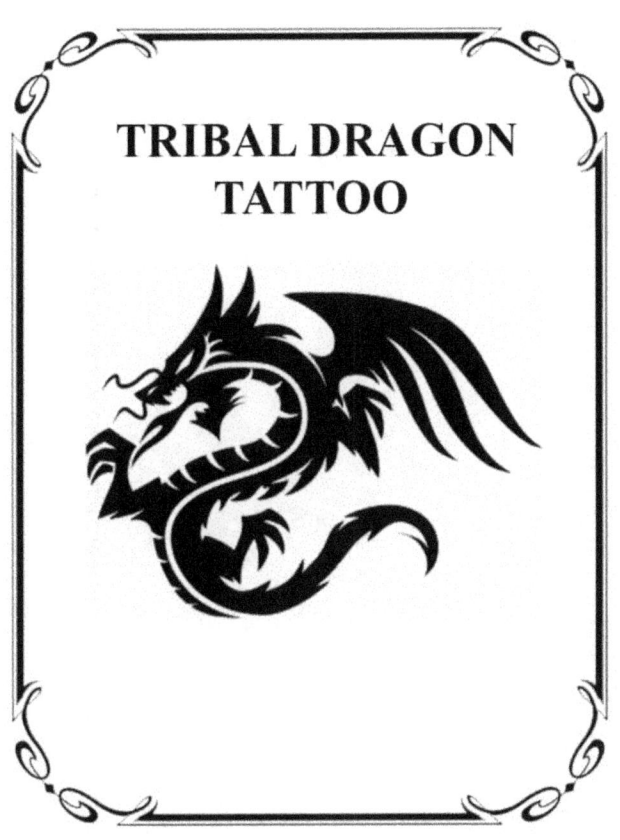

STEP 1

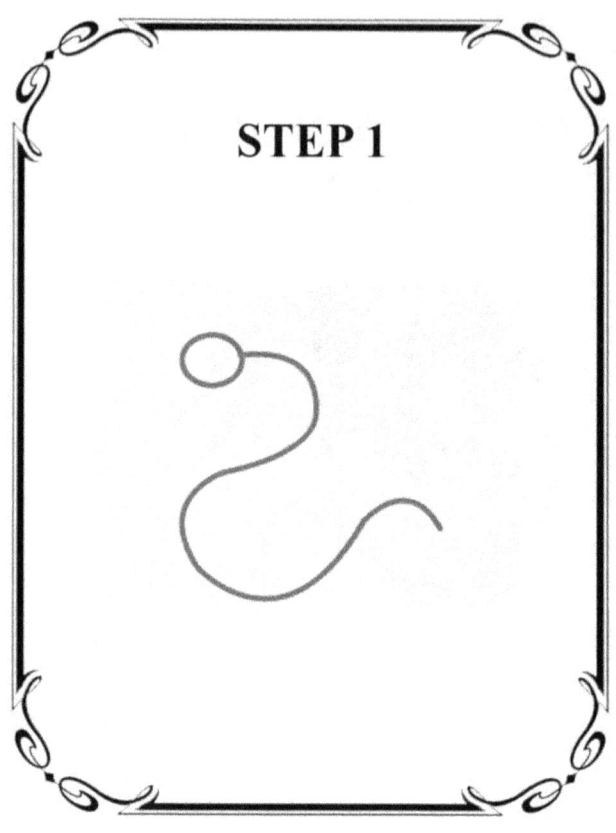

STEP 2

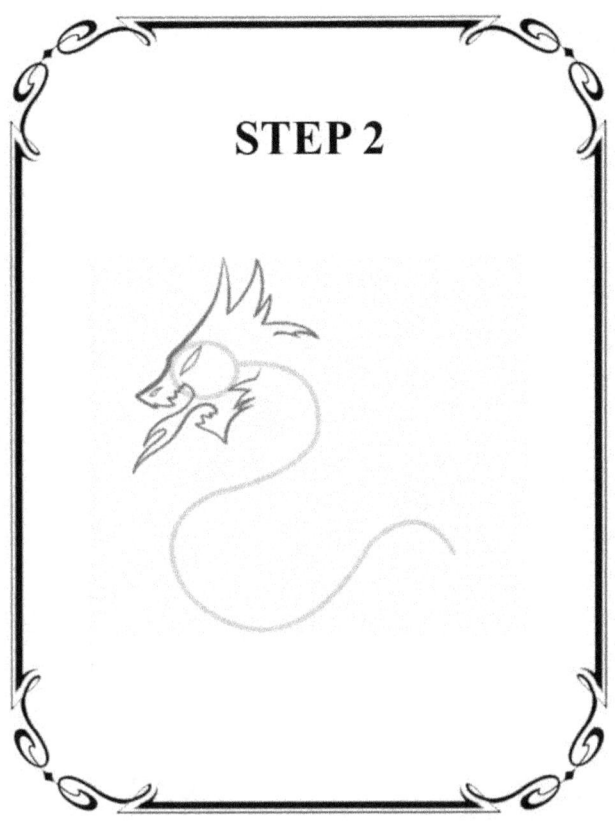

STEP 3

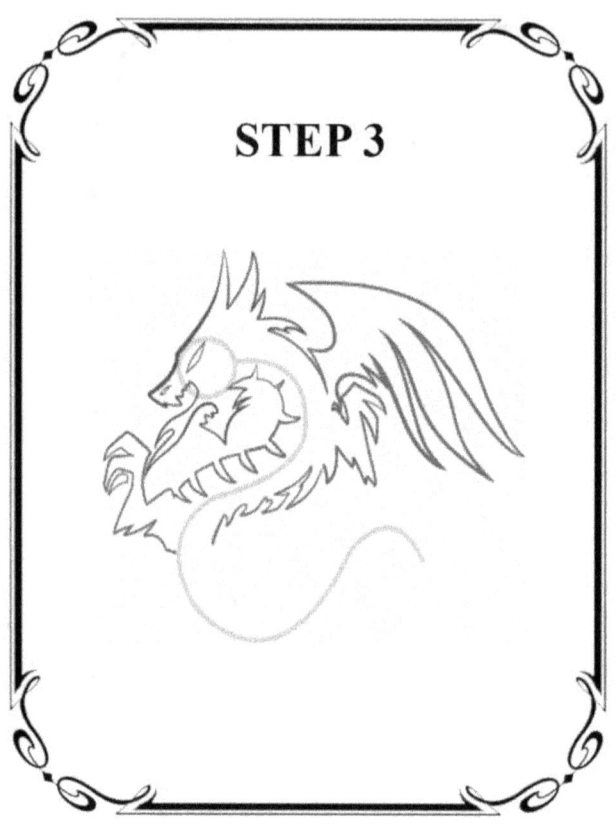

STEP 4

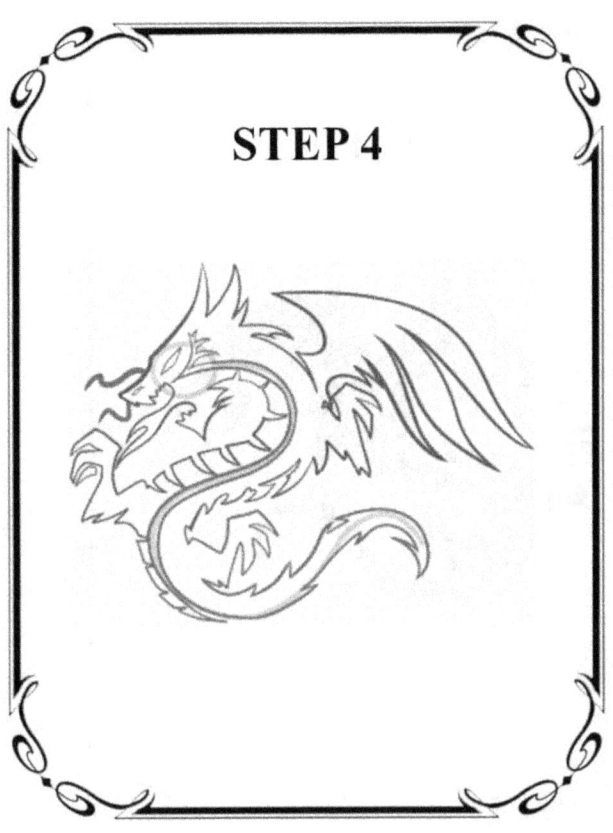

STEP 5

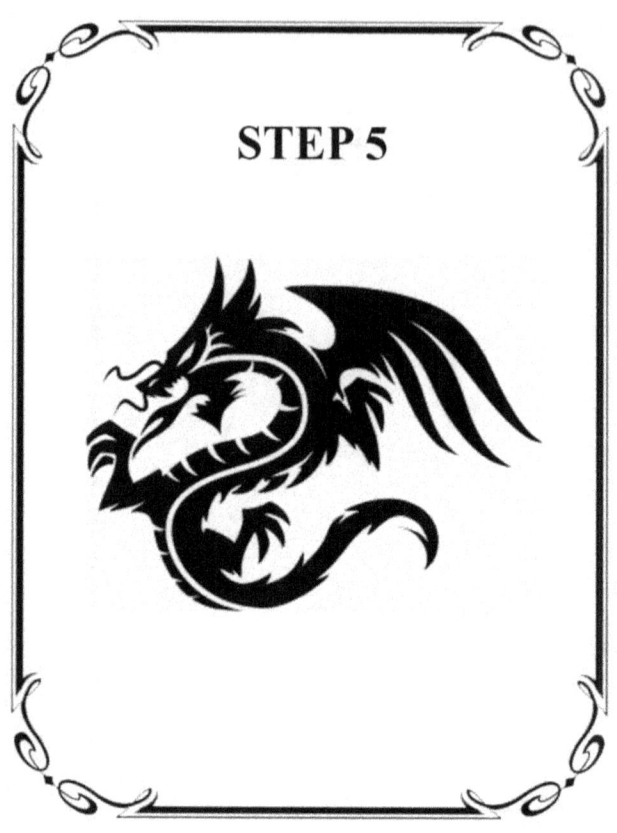